FEEL GOOD WITH

ADHD

BOOK FOR KIDS

An empowering guide with:

- ✓ engaging exercises
- ✓ quizzes
- ✓ and strategies

KARIN ROACH, MA, LMHC, CASAC

Illustrated by Kseniia Fast

AGES
8–12

R

**ROCKRIDGE
PRESS**

First Rockridge Press trade paperback edition 2022

Rockridge Press and the Rockridge Press logo are trademarks or registered trademarks of Callisto Media Inc. and/or its affiliates in the United States and other countries and may not be used without written permission.

For general information on our other products and services, please contact our Customer Care Department within the United States at (866) 744-2665, or outside the United States at (510) 253-0500.

Paperback ISBN: 978-1-68539-683-1
eBook ISBN: 978-1-63807-617-9

Manufactured in the United States of America

Interior and Cover Designer: Erik Jacobsen
Art Producer: Megan Baggott
Editor: Annie Choi
Production Editor: Nora Milman
Production Manager: Martin Worthington

Illustrations © 2022 Kseniia Fast

Author photo courtesy of Carla Phillips

10 9 8 7 6 5 4 3 2 1 0

Feel Good with ADHD Book for Kids

For my strong and lovely daughter, Delancey,
a bright star. You teach me so many things.

For H., along with all the adults who grew up
without the information to understand their ADHD.
May your experience help the kids of today.

CONTENTS

A LETTER TO KIDS

Welcome to your very own guide to what makes you uniquely YOU!

No two people are exactly the same—we all have different interests and abilities. Although one person may be skilled in one area, another person may need help doing the very same thing. This is totally natural! Similarly, having attention deficit hyperactivity disorder, or ADHD, means that your brain works in a certain way.

Do you find yourself distracted in school a lot? Do you forget your notebooks in class or leave important things at home? Do you sometimes miss instructions on homework? If you answered "yes" to any of these questions, that's okay! It just means you have a chance to work on certain skills. This book can help.

Here you will learn about ADHD. More importantly, you will learn about *your ADHD* and how it affects *you*. By completing the fun activities on the pages that follow, you will be armed with skills and strategies that can help you manage your ADHD and feel awesome about your unique qualities. Every time you complete the exercises in a chapter, you earn an Emotional Explorer badge. When you finish this book, you will have collected all six badges—and be well on your way to becoming an Emotional Explorer who can handle different kinds of emotions, big and small!

Along the way, you will learn how to manage your emotions, how to manage school and organization, how to handle arguments or disagreements, and how to set up your life to get things done at home. You will also gain some new social skills to better connect with friends and family.

This book is all yours, so write in it, draw in it, and circle and underline words. Let's help you shine!

Kindly,
Karin Roach

A LETTER TO GROWN-UPS

Welcome, grown-ups! You are taking a wonderful step toward empowering your child to thrive. This guide is for kids ages eight to twelve with ADHD. It will help them understand ADHD and feel good about themselves in the process. Please encourage your child to write and draw and engage in the interactive learning in this book—this book is theirs, after all.

In this book, I help kids develop skills to highlight their strengths and better self-regulate. Many other books tend to paint ADHD in a negative light, but this book takes a more positive approach—we all respond better to rewards than to punishment and negativity (you may already use a rewards chart or other forms of positive reinforcement such as calling out good behavior; if so, bravo!). This book will help your child understand that ADHD is part of what makes them the unique and amazing person they are. Kids with ADHD will see that they are smart and capable, not *less than*.

Throughout this book, I give your child examples they can relate to along with thirty-six exercises, fun quizzes, and prompts to explore and learn about ADHD. Kids will be given tools to help. Through the interactive exercises, kids will learn to manage their ADHD more effectively and to self-regulate, as well as build executive functioning skills, which allow them to plan ahead, maintain focus, and juggle different tasks.

Your child will learn what ADHD is, but more important, they will get to know themselves and how their ADHD affects them. This book uses evidence-proven methodology for all the exercises and tips, including cognitive behavioral therapy (CBT), mindfulness, and dialectical behavioral therapy (DBT) skills for emotional dysregulation. CBT helps kids recognize unhelpful thoughts and behaviors. It gives kids tools for changing thoughts and behaviors that are not working well. Mindfulness is used in tandem with CBT to teach calming techniques and how to be in the present moment and not be stuck in the past or worry about a potential future. DBT skills help kids manage extreme emotions and self-regulation.

Your child is a unique, dynamic individual who is growing and developing all the time. You clearly want to support your child in the best way possible to be their happiest, most confident self. You are both on your way!

Kindly,
Karin Roach

All about ADHD

In this chapter, we start exploring ADHD and how it affects many areas of life, in some ways helpful and in other ways challenging. You'll find a bunch of exercises that are designed to uncover skills you already have and also to help you develop new skills. Along the way, you will earn badges in order to become an Emotional Explorer. Ready to begin?

What Is Attention Deficit Hyperactivity Disorder?

Attention deficit hyperactivity disorder, or ADHD, is a name for a set of behaviors that many kids and grown-ups have. People who have ADHD can't help having these behaviors, but they can learn how to manage them. When you know that you have ADHD, then you, your parents, and your teachers understand why you sometimes have difficulty focusing or staying still.

The **attention deficit** part means it is hard to focus on many steps and that you can get distracted. You are smart and knowledgeable, but attention deficit gets in the way of finishing homework, for example.

Most kids are active and like running, climbing, and jumping. **Hyperactivity** means constantly being active, and if you have the hyperactive type of ADHD, you may have a hard time stopping, even when you are told to stop.

Kids with ADHD are smart, talented, and creative— this includes you! ADHD is not all of who you are. Many pieces make up your personality. We will explore your special talents. You will identify your superpowers, such as multitasking, which means doing many things at the same time, or hyperfocus, which means focusing on something for a long time.

Are there people you know with ADHD? Yes! Amazing athletes like Olympic gymnast Simone Biles and swimmer Michael Phelps along with celebrities like singer Justin Timberlake and astronaut Scott Kelly all have ADHD.

Are These Things I Might Do?

Put a check mark next to any of the following things that describe you:

- ❑ I have trouble staying organized, and it is hard to keep track of homework.

- ❑ Sometimes I miss part of the homework.

- ❑ Sometimes my mind wanders in class even when I am trying to pay attention.

- ❑ I am always running late to get out the door, even when I try to stay on a schedule.

- ❑ I avoid things that take a lot of time, like schoolwork or chores.

- ❑ I often lose pencils, books, glasses, or toys.

- ❑ I have a hard time sitting still for a long time. At school, I squirm in my seat or try to get out of class.

If you checked off three or more of these things, then this book can help you. You can develop skills to manage these behaviors and do well in school, at home, and with friends.

Everyone Is Different

Dashawn is often late getting to class. When the teacher calls for students to get out their notebooks and pencils, Dashawn takes a long time because his backpack is messy, and he left his pencils at home. During recess, Dashawn leaves soccer games because he gets bored. Dashawn has the **inattentive type** of ADHD.

Andy likes to climb a lot, even up the fence outside school. In class, Andy sometimes blurts out an answer to a question when it's not his turn. Andy can be really funny, but sometimes Andy is told to stop because it is not the right time for a joke. Andy has the **hyperactive-impulsive type** of ADHD.

Sophia writes down some of the homework, but she forgets to write down *all* of it, so she misses some of what is due. She does not like to read for a long time at school, so Sophia goes to the bathroom during silent reading time. She is also thoughtful and helpful to friends in need. Sophia has the **combined type** of ADHD. This is the most common type.

Are you most like Dashawn, Andy, or Sophia? Knowing which kid you are most like will help you find which areas to concentrate on.

What Does ADHD Look Like to Me?

Take this quiz to find out which parts of ADHD you are experiencing. Circle each one that describes you.

1. I forget things I need for school.

2. My backpack and locker are usually messy.

3. Sometimes I miss part of the instructions and don't finish a school assignment without a reminder.

4. I avoid chores or too much homework.

5. I lose things like pencils, school assignments, or books.

6. I climb or squirm a lot, even when I'm supposed to be still.

7. I interrupt when someone is talking.

8. I talk a lot and sometimes people tell me to stop.

9. It's really hard for me to wait my turn in line.

10. I don't like to play alone.

If you answered only numbers 1, 2, 3, 4, or 5: You may be most like Dashawn. Dashawn has the **inattentive type** of ADHD.

If you answered only numbers 6, 7, 8, 9, or 10: You might be most like Andy. Andy has the **hyperactive-impulsive type** of ADHD.

If you answered some from numbers 1, 2, 3, 4, or 5 and some from numbers 6, 7, 8, 9, or 10: You may be most like Sophia. Sophia has the **combined type** of ADHD.

Why Do I Have ADHD?

You didn't get ADHD because you ate too much candy or played too many video games. In fact, you didn't do *anything* to get ADHD. Scientists don't know all the reasons why some kids have ADHD, but they do know that it may run in your family, similarly to brown or green eyes, or curly or straight hair. Just like you can learn to take care of your curly hair, you can also learn to manage certain behaviors that come with ADHD.

Both kids and grown-ups have ADHD. Some grown-ups don't know why they lose things, talk too much, or have big feelings. They never learned about their ADHD when they were young. You are learning to understand your ADHD now, and that is going to be really useful. You can learn why the behaviors and big feelings happen and how to prepare for them. You can use these skills to tell grown-ups what is happening.

Now that you are learning about ADHD, you can understand it and explain it to your teachers, parents, and even friends. When the people around you understand, they can help you learn in the way that works best for you. Many successful people have used their ADHD to help them hyperfocus, be more creative, and much more. You can learn to use your ADHD as a superpower, too.

BE MINDFUL: ROBOT TO NOODLE

It is natural to get sad, upset, or stressed out about your ADHD. The Robot to Noodle exercise helps calm your body, which also calms your mind. Try it!

Breathe in and make your arms into steel, tense up your legs and feet, and make your face hard. Be a robot for a count of three. Next, release all the tension and blow out of your mouth—*phew*. Be like a noodle and swing your noodle arms side to side.

My ADHD Skills

You are already using your own skills to manage your ADHD. Identify any of the skills that you know or use by filling in the blanks below.

1. I know I need a break when _____. The appropriate way to take the break is to _____ _____.

2. My favorite way to exercise is _____. Another good way that I can get my energy out is _____.

3. When I am feeling frustrated, I feel it in this part of my body most: _____.

4. In order to calm myself, I _____ (check all the phrases that apply):

❏ Take three deep breaths

❏ Help others

❏ Do jumping jacks

❏ Count to ten

❏ Play with a fidget tool

❏ Splash cold water on my face

❏ Play a video game

❏ Chew on a chew tool

Draw a picture of yourself using your favorite calming method.

ADHD and My Life

ADHD can affect different parts of your life, so that is why this book is divided into different areas, like school, home, family, friends, and the larger community.

At school, ADHD can affect your grades, for example, because sometimes you know the answers but have trouble finishing the schoolwork. You might forget to do part of your work. Sometimes you lose things that you need.

ADHD can have an effect on your friends. Friends might want to play a game, but you get bored easily and want to leave before the game is finished.

At home, your mom or dad may ask you to clean up your room and finish your homework. They might think you're not listening and get frustrated, which makes you feel upset. ADHD often comes with big feelings that are hard to control.

In this book, we will work together to figure out which areas in your life are most affected by ADHD. You'll find many tips along the way. You will learn strategies and new skills and even earn badges.

Just like practicing a musical instrument or riding a bike, practicing new behaviors can make difficult things easier in school, at home, or during play.

YOU'VE GOT THIS!
CALM BREATHING

When you start feeling big emotions, try this easy breathing exercise. Once you learn it, you will be able to calm your body and focus your mind.

Breathe in through your nose for a count of four. Then blow out through your mouth—like blowing out birthday candles—for a count of eight. Do that breathing four times in a row, then breathe normally.

Good work calming yourself down!

What Are My Strengths?

Put a check mark next to the things that describe you:

❏ I am kind to my friends.

❏ I am good at art/music.

❏ I am funny.

❏ I have teachers I really like.

❏ I am good at science.

❏ I am a writer.

❏ I am good at technology.

❏ I am good at math.

❏ I play a sport.

❏ I like spending time with my family.

❏ I have a pet.

❏ I am a leader.

❏ Other: _____

If you checked any of these, then you already have focus, empathy, kindness, leadership, or sharp wits. Let's build on these!

Real Problems, Real Solutions

Let's look at some examples of real-life problems and their solutions.

Problem: *You are having a difficult time paying attention because your classmate keeps talking.*

Solution: *Politely ask the teacher to write the instructions.*

Problem: *You got frustrated with your homework and quit.*

Solution: *Take a break and use a calming skill, then come back.*

Problem: *Your mom tells you to do homework and you get mad and slam the door.*

Solution: *Use a calming skill such as coloring or drawing. Let your mom know when you are ready.*

Problem: *You left your weekly planner with homework assignments at school.*

Solution: *Ask your trusted grown-up if they can help you find out what the homework is.*

Congratulations!
You have earned your first badge.

Me and My ADHD

You are unique and so is your ADHD. You may experience some of the same feelings as other kids with ADHD, but some of your feelings will be different. In this chapter, you will learn how to identify your emotions and which ones get big quickly. You will also learn how to better manage those big emotions.

Learning to Self-Regulate

Do you ever feel yourself getting mad or sad quickly? Emotions can be like the temperature on a thermometer. They can go from cold to hot really quickly. When your emotions get really big really fast, they can affect your behavior or even your body.

Here is an example: Ashley was almost done with her math homework when she noticed that there was a whole other page of work. She got frustrated and thought, *I hate math. Why do I even have to do this?* She crumpled up her paper and threw it on the floor. Ashley was having a hard time self-regulating.

Here's another example: Javier had difficulty with self-regulating at basketball practice. He was able to play for a bit, but then the coach told him to sit on the bench so others could play. Javier thought, *I will never be good if I don't get to play more*, and then he started to cry.

Feelings are good to have, but sometimes they become too big and overwhelming. The good news is that self-regulation is something you can work on. Once you learn to regulate your feelings, you can better use the thinking part of your brain.

Managing My Emotions

Everybody gets mad, sad, and scared. People feel a lot of in-between emotions and mixed emotions, too. Can you think of a time when you were a little bit scared and a little bit excited? Like before an event that you were looking forward to?

Part of self-regulating is managing emotions. Sometimes when kids run into challenges, they can get stressed out or angry, whether they have ADHD or not. This is totally normal. Having ways to manage emotions is a big help in managing other obstacles. If you get mad and act out, you could make someone else upset, and then you both feel bad.

Does the following scenario sound familiar? Javier went to school after staying up too late the night before, and he skipped breakfast. He found out that his desk had been moved and his pencil was missing. Javier got upset, refusing to sit in the desk and angrily storming out of class. Ms. Selma at the front office helped Javier calm down with a stress tool and a snack. When Javier returned to class, his teacher warned him not to leave during the lesson. Javier did not want to tell his mom about leaving class. He wished he could have calmed down sooner and told himself that next time he would practice Calm Breathing (page 13).

My Feelings Thermometer

Let's take a look at how you view your own feelings. Write down your feelings (*happy, worried, annoyed,* or whatever you call your feelings) on the left side of the thermometer closest to the color that best matches that feeling.

For example, when you are in the green zone, you are *happy, calm,* and *not worried.* When you are in the yellow zone, you are neither happy nor sad, calm nor excited. When you are in the red zone, you are either very mad, very sad, in a panic (very scared), or too excited.

On the right side, write down some behaviors that happen when you are in the different zones. For example, if you wrote "very angry" in the red zone, maybe a behavior that came from that is that you decided to throw something across the room.

Remember, it is okay to be honest about what happens, even if you feel bad about it. You will build skills to make changes to behaviors that you don't want to do.

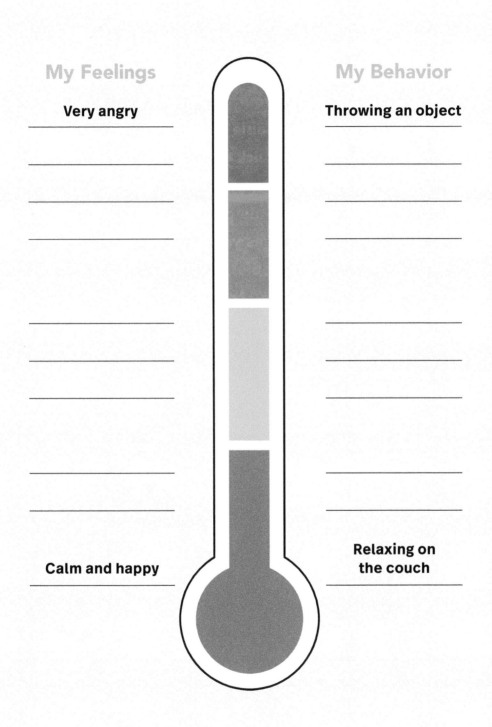

My Feelings

Very angry

Calm and happy

My Behavior

Throwing an object

**Relaxing on
the couch**

BE MINDFUL: MOVE MY BODY
TO CHANGE MY MIND

When you notice your feelings are getting too big and you are able to take a break in a safe space, get some quick exercise. Can you find a place to do ten jumping jacks? Or skip? Or dance? If you are outside or in the gym, take a running break. Exercising changes your brain in good ways. Exercise makes you happier, calmer, and more focused. Exercise is good to do every day, and it is especially helpful in changing your angry feelings to calmer feelings when they are happening. Pick whatever exercise that you like to do.

How Well Do I Manage My Emotions?

Let's see where your emotions are and how you are managing them. Circle either A, B, or C.

1. I can calm myself down when I am mad or upset.

    a. Often

    b. Some of the time

    c. Rarely

2. When I am asked to do a new task or project, I think about all the bad parts of it.

    a. Rarely

    b. Some of the time

    c. Often

3. When I get excited or mad or scared, I can make myself think of something else.

    a. Often

    b. Some of the time

    c. Rarely

4. People say I am moody or intense.

   a. Rarely

   b. Some of the time

   c. Often

5. I feel really bad when someone criticizes something I have done.

   a. Rarely

   b. Some of the time

   c. Often

If you answered mostly As, then you are noticing your big feelings. You have skills and are already practicing using them. Good job! We will cover some more skills, because it is good to have a lot to choose from.

If you answered mostly Bs, then you are noticing your feelings and are starting to manage them using the skills that you have. Keep it up! You will learn even more ways of managing your big feelings in this book.

If you answered mostly Cs, then you may need more practice. Keep reading and writing in this book, because you will gain a lot of new skills to help manage these big feelings.

Knowing My Triggers

Have you ever used a squirt gun? If you have, you know that when you squeeze the trigger, water squirts out and you get your friends wet (which *is* really fun and feels good on a hot summer day). We all have things that trigger emotions or responses. The squirt gun trigger makes water soak someone, whereas emotional triggers can make emotions happen.

There are things that trigger us to act in certain ways. When the ice-cream truck plays a song (the trigger), we go toward the sound and get an ice cream (the behavior/response). Some things trigger behaviors that we don't want. For example, when you pull the wrong piece out in a Jenga block game (trigger), all the pieces fall (the behavior/response).

For kids and grown-ups with ADHD, there are some common triggers that bring on big emotions that are hard to control. These common triggers include not getting enough sleep, hunger, getting overwhelmed with too many steps, feeling lonely, or someone criticizing you.

Remember the story of Javier getting mad when someone moved his desk and pencil? Javier had a few triggers, such as not sleeping enough and not eating breakfast.

After you have calmed down from a big emotion, you can think about what happened *before* it and write that down. If you do this a bunch of times, you may discover your own personal triggers. You can keep your list of triggers in a notebook or on a computer or phone that you use all the time.

Try the exercise on the next page to investigate your triggers.

My Triggers

Take a look at this list. Put a check mark next to the moments and things that happen during your day that can significantly affect your mood and emotions:

❑ Not getting enough sleep

❑ Hunger

❑ A change in routine

❑ Being criticized

❑ An upcoming test

❑ Being on a screen for too long

❑ Classmates leaving me out

❑ Not getting a turn

❑ Being embarrassed

❑ Being assigned a lot of homework

❑ Having to sit quietly

❑ A certain kind of food

❑ Loud music

Good work beginning to identify your triggers!

Building My Self-Esteem

Is there something you are good at? When you do something you are good at, you trust that you will be able to do it. This is called having self-esteem. Having healthy self-esteem is a big part of being successful—whether you have ADHD or not.

When we struggle with things, like being on time or getting homework done, it can make us feel frustrated and sad. This can lower our self-esteem. However, building self-esteem can help us do better in school, at home, with friends, or anywhere else in the world.

Here is an example of how self-esteem can help: Essence and Nasir were both asked to come up with an idea for the science fair. Essence really liked studying how human muscles work, and Nasir was interested in marine biology. Nasir considered doing a project on whales, but then thought he would not have time to make it perfect and people might make fun of it, so he decided not to submit a project. Essence had an idea to show how muscles work by using a big rubber band. She did not know exactly how it would turn out. Still, Essence assembled the project and presented it to the teacher. She was picked for the science fair! Essence's healthy self-esteem and trust in herself led to her getting this cool honor.

Science Fair

How did self-esteem affect Essence and Nasir? Circle *true* or *false* after each of the following statements. In the blanks that follow, write about your experience.

Both Essence and Nasir had a chance to be in the fair.

TRUE   FALSE

Nasir should have presented his idea.

TRUE   FALSE

It is usually better to go for it if there is a new task or skill you want to try.

TRUE   FALSE

Self-esteem can affect your choices. It is good to have healthy self-esteem.

TRUE   FALSE

A time when I tried something that was hard for me was:

_____

_____

_____.

Afterward, I remember feeling:

_____

_____

_____.

Real Problems, Real Solutions

Problem: *You are late to class and the teacher gives you a tardy slip. You feel yourself getting angry.*

Solution: *Find a quiet place to sit down and begin doing Calm Breathing (page 13).*

Problem: *Kids are not picking you to play a game in the park. You feel like you might yell at them.*

Solution: *Take a run around the area.*

Problem: *You have a lot of homework, which is one of your triggers.*

Solution: *Good job identifying the trigger (see page 27)! Take a break and come back.*

Problem: *You keep forgetting your planner or notebook at school.*

Solution: *Tape a reminder note to the last place that you look before you go home.*

Congratulations!

You've earned another badge.

Me at School

School can be exciting, but it also brings challenges for kids who have ADHD. In this chapter, you will explore and discover where your strengths are in school and where you might need to get some skills. We will explore things like organization and refocusing. Let's try it out!

Real Kids Like Me

Mariah, Fatimah, and José all use special skills to manage school challenges.

Mariah's teacher tells the class to take out their notebooks and pencils. Mariah takes out her notebook but only has an old pen with no ink. She forgot to bring a pencil to school. Mariah remembers that her teacher helped her *plan ahead* for times like this. She and her teacher left pencils in her locker for times when she doesn't have one. Mariah gets a pencil from her locker and begins the first assignment.

Fatimah stayed late in math class to catch up on an assignment when she heard the bell ring for science class to start. Fatimah learned to take a *brain break* when transitions happened. She told the teacher she needed to take a short bathroom break and then rejoin the class.

José's teacher gave the class an assignment to fill out a graphic organizer. José did not want to do this, and he was talking loudly instead. When the teacher told José to refocus, José remembered that he could *break the work into smaller parts.* He decided to try to write just the first line. It felt good to begin, and José was then able to complete the next line.

Make a Backpack Flash Card

With just a few simple steps, you can make a helpful tool that you keep in your backpack so you won't forget things you need for school!

1. Find an index card in your favorite color.

2. Make a list of items you need. Ideas include:

   - ❏ Pencils/pens
   - ❏ Eraser
   - ❏ Notebooks
   - ❏ Anything else you need!

3. Decorate the flash card with colors and stickers if you want.

4. Place the flash card somewhere in your backpack so that you will remember it.

5. Refer to the card in the morning before you head out the door to school.

Bonus: Take a picture of the card with a phone or tablet, or have a guardian take a picture. That way, you can have someone else help remind you.

1.

2.

3.

4.

5.

Settling into the School Day

Sometimes we can feel overwhelmed with everything we need to remember in the morning at school, and this is totally normal. Routines can help keep you grounded.

Remember Mariah from the Real Kids Like Me section of this chapter (page 34)? Before Mariah kept extra supplies in her locker, she would miss some of the class notes and homework assignments. Mariah learned to handle her challenge by planning ahead with a trusted grown-up. You can do this, too! Here are three strategies that you can use to start your day feeling great.

NIGHT-BEFORE STRATEGY: Set an alarm for after dinner to lay out the clothes you will wear the next day. You can repack your backpack with a binder, notebooks, books, and pencils at that time, too.

MORNING GET-READY LIST: Make a list of all the things you need to do before you leave the house. Put the list in a place where you will see it when you get up (bedside or bathroom wall). This can also be your Backpack Flash Card (page 36).

SET A TWO-ALARM STRATEGY: Set an alarm to wake up in the morning. Set a second alarm five minutes before you have to leave to remind you and your guardian that it's time to go out the door.

BE MINDFUL: USE A MANTRA

A *mantra* is something you say over and over in your mind to remember. Use a mantra in the morning to help you stay on track and get to class on time. Something like *I'll be on time to science class.* Repeat your mantra in your mind as you make your way to class.

My School Morning

Fill in the blanks to describe your morning routine.

The way that I get to school is _____

(walk, school bus, car, train/city bus). I need to be in

school at _____ (time). When I get to my class, the

first thing I do is _____. I open my backpack or

desk and take out my _____. I keep my sup-

plies in my _____.

    The hardest thing for me in the morning is

_____. The thing that I like best at school is

_____. I get distracted by _____. I get settled

in best when I _____.

    I have a grown-up who can help me organize; that

person is _____.

    One way that I could improve my morning routine is

to _____.

Inside the Classroom

Sometimes kids with ADHD are trying their best to pay attention in class, but they feel like they can't help but think about anything and everything else. Or they feel like they have ants in their pants. José had this challenge when his teacher told him he was supposed to write an essay. He kept talking loudly, and his brain was telling him that this essay would take too long, and it was way too hard to start.

José remembered a strategy that he learned to help him get going on his essay. Learning how to focus and actively pay attention is a skill just like learning to ride a bike, do a dance move, or shoot a basketball. You can train your brain just like you train your muscles. Here are some strategies to help:

THE BREAK-IT-DOWN STRATEGY: Do a portion of the assignment and then stop to take a break for a few minutes. For an essay, write a little bit in a graphic organizer. For math problems, do one or two problems and then take a break. You can go back and do more later, but breaking it down makes it less overwhelming.

THE REMINDER STRATEGY: Ask the teacher to give you a written reminder of the verbal assignment they gave the class (this could be written on the board or on a piece of paper). If you are working with a classmate, ask that person to write it.

THE FIDGET TOOL STRATEGY: You can use a fidget tool, stress ball, or chew tool to help you stay focused. Get these from a parent, guardian, or school counselor.

What parts of the class do you need to focus on most?

Managing School-Day Challenges

Circle the letter that best represents the way you would choose to handle the school-day challenge presented.

1. You're running late to class because a friend stopped you in the hall to chat. You:

   a. Get mad at the friend for making you late and start arguing with them.

   b. Stop talking to your friend, go to class, and tell the teacher it was your friend's fault.

   c. Remember a mantra (get to class) and tell your friend you'll talk later.

2. You just finished a bunch of math problems and still have a long reading assignment left to do. You:

   a. Keep going even though you can't focus.

   b. Yell out, "This is way too much work!"

   c. Ask to take a brain break.

3. You have a four-paragraph essay to write. You:

   a. Rush and write only two paragraphs.

   b. Ignore the assignment and fall asleep.

   c. Use a graphic organizer to organize your thoughts and ideas.

If you answered Cs, way to go! If you answered As or Bs, thanks for being honest. Let's learn more skills!

School Supplies and Organization

Organization is super helpful for kids with ADHD, and it is a skill that can be practiced. When Mariah did not set up her backpack with the things she needed, she missed writing down some of her homework and did not get it done. Getting organized helps exercise what's called the "executive functioning" part of your brain.

When you think of the executive functioning part of the brain, think about Boss Brain. Boss Brain likes to organize and run things by remembering, being flexible, and not getting distracted. When you prepare for school, it will make you feel less stressed out. You won't get embarrassed by not having what you need. You also won't need to try to catch up on things that you missed. Here are three strategies for getting organized.

MY BINDER STRATEGY: Organize your three-ring binder and planner with the tabs for the classes you will have, such as Math, Science, and ELA. If you have folders for these classes, put them in the binder under their proper sections. At the end of the day, file papers in the right section.

MY HOMEWORK PLANNER STRATEGY: Have a homework section at the front of your binder where you write the date and the homework for each class. Ask a teacher to double-check it at the end of the day.

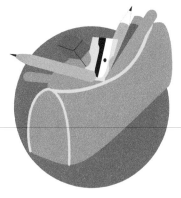

MY TOOLBOX STRATEGY: Get a pencil case or box and make sure it has two or three pencils, two pens, a sharpener, and an eraser in it. Restock and tidy it up.

YOU'VE GOT THIS!
KEEP IT SIMPLE

You don't need a lot of pens and pencils and notebooks. You just need something to write with and something to write on. The less you have to keep track of and keep organized, the less stressful it will be.

How Should I Set It Up?

What sections are in your binder? What are the items that you use every day in school that will need to go into your backpack? For a lot of people, writing something down and seeing it helps them remember better. In the space below, make a list of all the items that you need to make sure you have in your backpack. (If you did the Backpack Flash Card exercise on page 36, you already have your list. If not, you can do it now.)

My Supply List

_____

_____

_____

_____

_____

_____

Draw a picture of the items you included in your supply list.

Real Problems, Real Solutions

Problem: *You aren't sure if you have everything you need in the morning before you leave home.*

Solution: *Check your backpack list (see page 46) and look in your backpack. Grab what you need.*

Problem: *A classmate wants to show you a cool new game, but class is starting.*

Solution: *Use your mantra (see page 38) to remind yourself that this is the time to get to class.*

Problem: *You are having a hard time paying attention to the teacher.*

Solution: *Use Calm Breathing (page 13) to calm your mind.*

Problem: *You look in your desk for a pencil and there is nothing to write with.*

Solution: *Check your backpack and locker. If there are none, ask to borrow one. Say, "Thank you."*

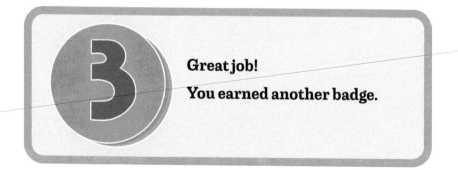

3

Great job!

You earned another badge.

Me at Home

Home should be a safe and comfortable space, but there are also some challenges for kids with ADHD. As you grow up, you will gain more independence and more responsibilities at home. Read on for some cool exercises to help strengthen your executive functioning muscles, or Boss Brain (see page 43), and get into helpful routines.

Real Kids Like Me

Matt's dad told him that he expects him to clean up his room. When Matt's dad comes to check his room, Matt has already moved on to playing a video game. The socks that he arranged are neat and tidy, but the rest of the room still looks messy. Matt and his dad make a poster for cleaning, including what needs to be done in what order and with lots of pictures.

Hakeem feels like he gets a boost of energy at night. When it is time for bed, Hakeem wants to work on a comic he is drawing because he has a lot of ideas for it. The ideas and thoughts seem to pop into Hakeem's head right at bedtime. Hakeem's grandma helped him download an app with soothing meditation music. It helps Hakeem practice letting his brain relax. He listens to it when it is time to wind down for sleep.

Ashley couldn't find her new headphones and felt sad and mad about it. She threw her clothes around her bedroom. Once she calmed down, Ashley asked her mom to help look for her headphones. They straightened up her room and found the headphones under the bed. They installed a special hook on the wall for Ashley to hang her headphones on whenever she comes into her room.

Where I'm Strong and Where I'm Still Practicing

Put a check mark next to the things that you do well at home and underline things that you need to practice.

☐ I do some chores.

☐ I can get to sleep close to bedtime.

☐ I clean my room regularly.

☐ I can find lost items with a little help.

☐ I have a schedule.

☐ I help my family/guardians.

☐ I can get up in the morning with one reminder.

☐ I put my dishes in the sink.

☐ I brush my teeth without being asked.

If you checked any of the listed items, then you are already organized and contributing to your household. If you had a lot of underlined answers, that's fine. In the next pages, you will learn some great strategies to help you get organized and helping out at home.

Personal Spaces

It is important to feel comfortable and safe in your personal space at home. Kids with ADHD sometimes have trouble staying organized, and this can make activities feel uncomfortable and chaotic. In the Real Kids Like Me section on page 52, Ashley got frustrated and upset when she lost her headphones. She was happy to find them and built a special hook where she keeps them now.

Certain executive functioning skills, like organization and routine, can make a big difference and make home feel like a calmer, happier space. Here are some strategies to help you exercise your Boss Brain (see page 43).

ROOM-CLEANING CHECKLIST: Make a checklist of steps to clean your room. You can find examples on the internet or ask a guardian. Keep it simple and add drawings. **Bonus:** Take a picture of your clean room to look at for next time.

BEDTIME WIND-DOWN: Bedtime calming routines really help. Set a time to start winding down. First, turn off all screens for the night. Then read a book or draw for about 30 minutes. Finally, do some evening meditation or breathing exercises, or listen to soothing sleep music before you doze off.

PICK A SPECIAL SPOT: For the things that you want and need every day, like headphones, a favorite book, or glasses, pick a special spot as their "home." Maybe it is a hook on the wall or a small bin. You will know where to find them when you look.

When you have organization and routine, you are ready to explore!

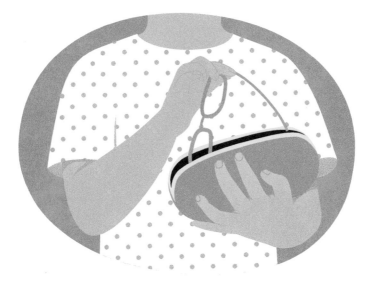

Bedroom Organization Challenge

In the list here, underline the five most important regular room-cleaning tasks. Remember, some things might be distractions.

1. Make the bed.

2. Play a round of Taco Cat Goat Cheese Pizza.

3. Put dirty clothes in the hamper and put away clean clothes.

4. Build a Minecraft world.

5. Pick up games and books and put them away.

6. Hang up a hammock.

7. Put away toys and equipment.

8. Train the cat to play piano.

9. Vacuum or sweep.

10. Do a TikTok dance.

If you picked 1, 3, 5, 7, and 9, then you got them all. If you picked any of the others, that's okay. Doing puzzles and brain teasers will help you develop executive functioning skills. Now you can take a two-minute dance break.

Getting Things Done

Home is a fun place, but there are also chores, cleaning, pet care, and homework to do. All these things require time management and planning skills, which can be challenging for kids with ADHD. It takes a lot of care and coordination!

Learning how ADHD affects time management and planning can help you finish homework and chores quicker and easier. Here are some strategies that can help.

HOMEWORK TIME: Set a time when you start and end homework each day, and put it on a calendar or whiteboard. Be sure to write each subject on a time block.

DON'T WAIT BUT DO TAKE BREAKS: It is easy to put off getting started, so set a homework alarm to begin. You can take a five-minute break when you need to, but make sure to always come back to it.

CHORES AND REWARDS: Work with an adult to set chore and homework assignments, and then make a rewards chart. Your rewards should be things you want but that are not expensive, like a favorite lunch or a little extra screen time.

Be Chill at Home

Circle the best answer for each scenario.

1. Your parent or guardian suggests adding *sweeping* to your chores. You:

    a. Argue that this is not the chore agreement.

    b. Refuse to do any sweeping, ever.

    c. Work with them on a schedule and fair rewards for a chore chart.

2. You have homework to finish, and your friends are outside. You:

    a. Stay seated and make doodles.

    b. Get mad, ball up the page, and throw it.

    c. Take an exercise break and then come back to it.

3. It's your turn to take out the trash. You:

    a. Say it's not your turn.

    b. Grab the trash but drag it through the house.

    c. Tie up the trash and properly dispose of it.

4. You get a reward if you wash the dishes. You:

    a. Avoid the kitchen.

    b. Do half and walk away.

    c. Do them all and get your reward.

If you answered with Cs, keep up the good work! If you answered As or Bs, go back to those and try again.

YOU'VE GOT THIS!
CREATE A COZY STUDY

Set up a cozy study cubby that is in a quiet space with a clean desk or table. When you start your work, have your notebook, homework list, pencils, sharpener, and tablet or computer handy if you need one.

Bonus: Write a homework checklist on a whiteboard and check off tasks as you go.

Morning Time, Night Time

When Matt gets up for school in the morning, he must get himself ready and out the door by 8 a.m. sharp. Matt's dad drops him at the bus stop and goes to work. Matt used to have a hard time getting dressed in time, and he would forget stuff that he needed for school. Matt had to practice time management by getting up and out on time. Like a very important rocket launch, each thing has to happen in time for blastoff (3-2-1 . . . blastoff!).

Hakeem learned the importance of having a routine at bedtime because he used to get a boost of energy at night. Kids with ADHD do better with a routine to remind their bodies that it is time for sleep. By using a routine, Hakeem found a way to train his brain to not get caught in ideas, worries, or thoughts when it was time for sleep.

Learning how your ADHD affects you in the morning and at night will help you plan smoother and calmer mornings and nights. You are getting good at understanding yourself! Some strategies that you already know are making a morning get-ready list (page 37), Calm Breathing (page 13), and winding down at night (page 54). You also may already know some yoga and meditation.

BE MINDFUL: KEEP A ROUTINE

At night, do some deep breathing and listen to calming music or a meditation. Picture yourself watching a flowing river. When you wake up, use your morning list to keep yourself on track. If you are taking too long, double-check the list.

Observe Your Thoughts

Take a moment to sit calmly on the floor or in a chair. Practice your Calm Breathing—in through your nose for four counts, out through your mouth for eight counts (see page 13). After doing that four times, keep your eyes closed for another two minutes and let your thoughts come and go. Don't get stuck on any thought; let it float by like a cloud. It is natural for thoughts to come; just practice letting them float by. If this is hard to do without help, you can find a kids' guided meditation online.

In the space provided, write down three things you can do to make your body calm.

_____

_____

_____

_____

Draw a picture of your thought clouds floating by, with your thoughts written in them.

Real Problems, Real Solutions

Problem: *You made a morning checklist, but you keep forgetting one item on the list, like socks.*

Solution: *Move that item to a better location; for instance, put your socks in your shoes.*

Problem: *You avoid chores and need a reminder.*

Solution: *Ask your adult to add a reminder to your reward chart.*

Problem: *Homework is not your favorite, so sometimes you put off starting it.*

Solution: *Set an alarm on your alarm clock or device. Leave yourself a note of encouragement in your homework area.*

Problem: *You made a room-cleaning chart, but the list got too long and confusing.*

Solution: *Check with your grown-up on what the top five tasks are. Get rid of the rest.*

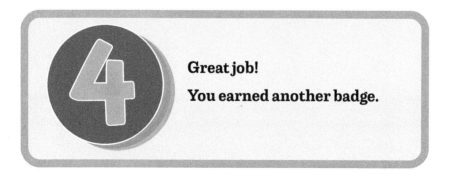

Great job!
You earned another badge.

Me with My Friends and Family

The time that you spend with your loved ones, family, and friends is something to cherish. Close friendships and family bonds can fill you with so much joy, but things aren't always perfect. In this chapter, you will do a fun exercise to find out your strengths and challenges, and you'll learn some great skills to manage the challenges. Let's go!

Real Kids Like Me

Mia likes to play her video game. When her mom told her that she needed to stop and wash up for dinner, Mia used to get mad and say mean things to her mom. Mia's mom used to get upset, and Mia felt bad afterward. She and her mom both learned that transitions from a fun activity are hard. They now have a plan in place with a five-minute warning.

Jayden wanted to join the soccer team because he liked playing with the kids on the team. During practice, however, there was a lot of waiting time for the ball to come down the field. Jayden would get so bored that he lost interest. After Jayden and his family learned that kids with ADHD have a harder time tolerating bore-dom, they decided to switch to a martial arts class where everyone was exercising the whole time.

My Strengths and Challenges with Family and Friends

Do you ever have a hard time with waiting? It is good to know that many kids and grown-ups are working on similar challenges. In the following list, put a check mark next to the items that are strengths for you and underline areas that are a challenge.

- ❏ Making art
- ❏ Controlling my impulses
- ❏ Building things
- ❏ Snuggling
- ❏ Baking
- ❏ Playing a sport
- ❏ Waiting my turn to talk

- ❏ Talking to new people
- ❏ Reading
- ❏ Singing
- ❏ Science
- ❏ Laser focus (sometimes)
- ❏ Being a leader

Write something *you* are good at that is not on this list:

_____.

Nice job getting to know your strengths and challenges!

Family

Family can be wonderful but also complicated. There are lots of different kinds of relationships between children and parents, siblings, grandparents, stepparents, adoptive families, or foster families. The kids in the beginning of this chapter are working through some challenges with their families.

Mia (who plays video games) sometimes gets upset with her mom, and her emotions go from low to high quickly. When Mia reaches her "boiling point," she knows she needs to take time to cool down.

It was confusing to Jayden's family when he wasn't interested in playing soccer after joining the team. They had to work together to understand.

Kylie's sister gets frustrated when Kylie doesn't wait to tell a story. Kylie and her grandma are working on it, and Kylie is able to apologize. Each of these kids is using a strategy.

Friends

It is wonderful to have all different kinds of friendships. Friendships can be supportive, and they can also be complicated. Mia has a friend who likes to follow the rules and keep her things very tidy, whereas Mia is more free-flowing and not so neat.

Jayden sometimes chews on his pencil erasers, and a couple of guys in his class called him a mean name. Jayden was able to play basketball with them and remind them that his name is Jayden.

Kylie interrupted a conversation between two of her school friends, and one of them called her rude. Kylie apologized and then took a break and played with someone else.

Kids and grown-ups with ADHD can learn to better understand social situations. Here are some strategies:

DIFFERENT IS OKAY: Your friend may be quite different from you and you both notice it. It is fine to enjoy the things you have in common and be okay with the things that are different.

MOVE ON: When a friend gets annoyed or says something not nice, remember that you can move on and not stay stuck. You can change behavior next time but let go of it for now. Choose to have a good rest of your day.

STOP AND COUNT TO 10: If you are about to say something and you get that feeling that it is not the right time, breathe deeply and count to 10. After that, decide if it is the right thing to say and/or the right time to say it.

What are the things you like about your friends?

Getting Along and Having Fun

Imagine a situation where you are playing a game or sport with a friend, family member, or classmate and you are doing a good job taking turns, playing together, and having fun.

Draw a picture of you in a situation where you're having fun with others.

Handling Conflict

As mentioned earlier, relationships can be hard some-times, especially when conflict happens. Conflict means a disagreement. It is important to know that conflict happens in all relationships. We read about the conflict between Mia and her mom over a video game, a name-calling conflict with Jayden, and a disruption conflict with Kylie and her sister. In each example, Mia, Kylie, and Jayden used different strategies to handle the conflict.

Understanding how your ADHD affects you when it comes to conflicts can help you handle it better and have fewer fights and more fun. You can have a normal disagreement without turning it into a fight. Here are some strategies to help:

TURN DOWN THE VOLUME: When you feel your thermometer going up (see page 20), practice making the volume of your voice go down. When you talk more softly, your brain calms down.

BE PREPARED: You have learned some of your triggers (see page 27), so get prepared for things that can be hard for you. When you have a transition at home or school, ask for a warning before the transition.

USE YOUR DETECTIVE SKILLS: Look for signs that someone is getting annoyed, such as a louder voice or annoyed face. Use Calm Breathing (page 13) when you detect these.

BE MINDFUL: VISUALIZE CALM

Use a glitter jar or snow globe, or just picture one in your mind. Shake it up. Do you see all the glitter or snow moving around? That is how your mind is working when you are upset. Wait until all of it settles back down. Now you are ready to move on.

What Would You Do?

Here are some scenarios involving conflict. Apply the tools that you have learned in the book so far and choose the best way to handle each scenario.

1. You accidentally shared a secret from a friend and now they are upset with you. You:

    a. Tell them they are being a baby.

    b. Apologize.

    a. Get upset, too, and yell.

2. Your mom gives you a five-minute warning to stop playing a video game. You:

    a. Wrap up the game and end it.

    b. Yell, "It's not fair!"

    c. Say that your friend plays for four hours.

3. You broke your aunt's coffee mug. You:

    a. Hide it.

    b. Tell her and offer to help fix it.

    c. Blame the dog.

4. A classmate called you rude for blurting out an answer. You:

   a. Tell them they are rude.

   b. Apologize and say that you are working on it.

   c. Make a face at them.

5. You didn't do a homework assignment and your parent found out. You:

   a. Admit it and try to make it up.

   b. Say you never knew about it.

   c. Say the dog ate it.

Were you able to choose the best answers? (They are B, A, B, B, A.) Great work!

Real Problems, Real Solutions

Problem: *A friend invites you to skate, and you exaggerated how good you are at it the week before.*

Solution: *Go skate anyway. If they ask you, let them know that you exaggerated.*

Problem: *You got upset with your dad when he told you to finish homework and you called him a name.*

Solution: *Tell him you need a break, and apologize later.*

Problem: *You go to your friend's piano recital, but your friend doesn't start until halfway through.*

Solution: *Ask your grown-up to let you step outside. They can get you when it's your friend's turn.*

Problem: *You want to get better at waiting your turn in school and at home.*

Solution: *Practice a game taking turns with your grown-up or counselor.*

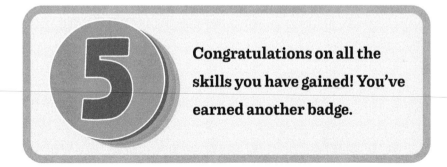

5 Congratulations on all the skills you have gained! You've earned another badge.

Me Out in the World

There are so many fun experiences out in the world, like birthday parties, sleepovers, hobbies, and sports. Some parts of these experiences can be challenging for kids with ADHD, and we will explore them in this chapter. We'll talk about fun strategies to build your social skills, like a detective debrief and making a video.

Real Kids Like Me

Elijah went to his friend Joe's birthday party. When Joe's cake came out, it was chocolate. Elijah prefers vanilla. Elijah yelled out, "Chocolate?! This stinks! Can't you get some vanilla?" After that, Joe did not want to sit next to Elijah when he was opening his presents. When Elijah got home, he and his mom talked about how things could have gone better.

Maddy liked to hang out in the park near school. When some school friends came, Maddy wanted them to play a game that she made up. She insisted that they stand in a certain spot and told them how to play it. After fifteen minutes, Maddy's school friends went to the swings and stopped playing Maddy's game. At first Maddy got annoyed, but then she decided to join them on the swings.

Aiden's teammates from soccer were celebrating after their team won. One of his teammates told Aiden he did a great job scoring a goal. Aiden replied, "Yeah, I did." Aiden thought things were fine, but his teammate walked off and stopped talking to him. Aiden's coach reminded Aiden to say, "Thank you" and "You did a great job, too." Aiden went to find his teammate to tell him that.

These real kids encountered some challenges but found positive ways to navigate them. Can you find the best way to navigate the following challenges?

Good-Behavior Sleuth

Using a pen or pencil, match the situation on the left with the description on the right:

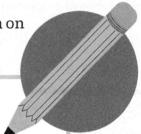

You walk into a friend's party and say, "Thank you for inviting me."

Not polite

You are at a movie theater and yell out to your friend.

Polite/ Appropriate

You don't want to play a game, so you say that it's boring and toss the pieces.

Too loud

You think your friend's shoes look old, but you don't say anything.

Thoughtful of others

Were you able to spot the polite and thoughtful behavior? Good job! Sometimes it's hard to control impulses, but it is good to try, especially when other people are involved.

Social Skills

As we grow up, we learn different social skills like listening, following directions, sharing, using manners, and cooperating with others.

Elijah worked on understanding that his friend liked chocolate better than vanilla. Elijah also recognized that he needed impulse control to not say the cake "stinks." Aiden was learning to use manners to say that his teammate played well, too. Maddy practiced sharing the choices of games.

Here are some ways you can practice your social skills:

SOCIAL SKILLS CHEAT SHEET: Make a social skills cheat sheet with a list of skills to practice every day. Keep it in a place you can check, and practice using the skills.

DETECTIVE DEBRIEF: After a social situation, like a birthday party, go over the events with a trusted grown-up. Check to see where things went right and where they may have gone wrong. You'll learn for the next time!

MAKE A SOCIAL SKILLS VIDEO: Make a video with a trusted grown-up or friend of two people using social skills like cooperation, manners, or listening.

Bonus: You can watch it when you need a reminder!

Savvy Social Skills

In the blanks that follow, write some social skills that you have used this week.

One time when I cooperated with someone in order to get something done was _____

_____.

Some ways that I use my manners are by _____

_____.

One time when I practiced good listening was (it can be with a family member, teacher, or friend) _____

_____

_____.

I followed directions when I _____

_____.

I was able to wait my turn when I _____

_____.

I apologized when I _____

_____.

If you were able to fill in any of the blanks, great work! Sometimes it's tougher to remember social skills in the moment, but you can look back at these answers and try to use some today.

Sleepovers, Hangouts, and Special Events

Fun things like sleepovers, hangouts, or going to an amusement park with friends can be awesome, but sometimes they can be challenging if you have ADHD.

Kids with ADHD might have difficulty getting to sleep at a sleepover, so they might need to prepare with a calming plan. Waiting in line at an amusement park might be frustrating. Birthday parties can sometimes be loud with unexpected events that you are not used to, which get overstimulating. Learning about your ADHD and how it affects your impulses and social skills can help you enjoy these fun events a lot more. Here are some useful strategies.

TALKING STICK: Practice using a talking stick (a custom of Indigenous Peoples in which only the person holding the stick is allowed to speak). When your friend or grown-up holds the stick, they talk and you listen. When you hold the stick, you talk and they listen.

ACT IT OUT BEFORE YOU GO: Role-play the event with a trusted adult. Go through what you will say and do during the different parts of the event. You can both play different roles. It will make it less uncomfortable during the real event.

BE A FRIEND DETECTIVE: When you are with strangers at an event, tell them your name and ask for their names. Try to remember their names, repeat them back, and also remember something that they like to do or talk about.

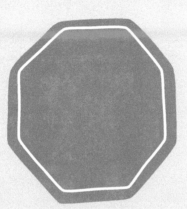

BE MINDFUL: STOP, LOOK, LISTEN

When you are at a special event, practice to *stop, look, listen.*

Stop talking for a minute.

Look around and make a mental note of what you see.

Listen to others talking and whatever other sounds you hear: birds, rain, music, anything.

This is a mindful practice you can use anywhere.

My Emotional Explorer Skills

Put a check mark next to the skills that you would like to get better at:

❑ Saying "thank you"

❑ Waiting my turn

❑ Complimenting others

❑ Helping others

❑ Cleaning up

❑ Not interrupting

❑ Being a friend

❑ Making people laugh

❑ Sharing with others

❑ Playing a board game

❑ Clearing my plate

❑ Asking for help

❑ Following directions

❑ Noticing if someone is sad

❑ Respecting personal space

You might be good at some of these already but need to work on others. That is totally normal! Everyone is unique. What might be harder for someone else could be easier for you, and what might be hard for you might be easier for someone else.

Activities and Hobbies

Part of everyday life includes after-school activities and hobbies. You might go to sports practice, ballet class, coding class, or even make videos with others. Let's revisit kids from earlier in the chapter.

Elijah got mad at losing in basketball and would storm off the court. He practiced taking a break and coming back to it. Maddy would get bored in ballet class because they would do the same movements over and over again. She took jumping breaks in between. Aiden was learning to play the guitar, but he did not like to practice. He tried doing a little bit every other day.

Learning about how your ADHD affects hobbies can help you enjoy them more. Here are some strategies:

BREAK IT DOWN: Limiting practices or drills to short time periods helps you stay on track. Do one exercise or practice and then move on to a different one.

LOSING IS PART OF LEARNING: Remember that you get better by making mistakes. You have to miss shots—or lose games—in order to get better and win.

PRETEND YOU ARE SOMEONE YOU ADMIRE: Pretend that you are someone who is really good at what you are doing. What would LeBron James, Beyoncé, or Lin-Manuel Miranda do?

YOU'VE GOT THIS!
PRACTICE MAKES PERFECT

Write a list of polite responses and practice saying them out loud, by yourself or with a grown-up. Things like: *Thank you. It's your turn. Could you help me with this?* Act them out. When you practice, they will come more easily when you need them!

What Do You Do?

Circle the letter for what you would do in the following situations.

1. In music, you have to wait a few minutes for the part that you play. You:

   a. Count, wait, and look at the teacher for a sign.

   b. Start doing something else.

   c. Play "Poker Face" instead.

2. Your team misses a shot in volleyball and loses the game. You:

   a. Yell out, "This is unfair!"

   b. Tell the other team, "Good game!"

   c. Storm off and quit volleyball.

3. At the amusement park, you want to go on the roller coaster first, but your friends want to go on the teacups first. You:

   a. Tell them they are babies.

   b. Refuse to go on the teacups.

   c. Go on the teacups, then the roller coaster.

4. You are playing tennis at camp, but the rules take too long to learn. Your opponent says you lost the game. You:

   a. Tell them they are wrong and walk off the court.

   b. Say okay, play the next game, and work on learning the basics.

   c. Get upset and say tennis is stupid.

5. You are at a friend's birthday with some kids you don't know. You:

   a. Play the games with them anyway and try to use their names.

   b. Ignore them and only talk to your friend with the birthday.

   c. Try to call your parent or guardian and ask them to come get you.

The best choices were A, B, C, B, A. Sometimes it's hard to make the right choices, but it is good to know what they are!

Real Problems, Real Solutions

Problem: *Gymnastics class is over and it's time to go home, but you want to keep going.*

Solution: *Do a transition routine of packing up gear and doing some Calm Breathing (page 13). Tell your grown-up about what you did in class.*

Problem: *You friends are playing a boring game at a birthday party.*

Solution: *Step away for a break to get a drink of water or a fidget tool.*

Problem: *Everyone is ready to go to sleep at a sleepover, but you are not sleepy.*

Solution: *Practice your wind-down routine (see page 54). Use a sleep mask, quiet music, or meditation.*

Problem: *You feel embarrassed after walking out of last week's soccer game.*

Solution: *Go to the game. Let your coach know that you may need a break during the game.*

Problem: *You told everyone you were good at kickball, but you only played once.*

Solution: *Let them know that you need a refresher, and you haven't played in a while.*

Congratulations!
You have earned all six badges. You are well on
your way to mastering your emotions!

Thank you for taking this journey. I hope that you have come away with some new skills to better manage your ADHD. You can look back at this book any time you want as a reminder of all the things you have learned! Your Boss Brain is still developing right now, and you will get even better at using your skills.

Best of luck on your journey, Emotional Explorer!

ACKNOWLEDGMENTS

Thank you, David, for always encouraging and inspiring me in all things creative. Thanks to Mom and Dad for teaching me to value the journey. Many thanks to Alyson and Matt for making this much-needed book happen.

ABOUT THE AUTHOR

 **Karin Roach, MA, LMHC, CASAC,** is a licensed mental health counselor and an internationally credentialed alcohol and substance abuse counselor with a private practice in New York City. She ran a groundbreaking inpatient treatment program for substance abuse and mental health for more than ten years. She is a producer for several award-winning films.

CPSIA information can be obtained
at www.ICGtesting.com
Printed in the USA
BVHW052343030622
637830BV00006B/8

9 781685 396831